CHRISTOPHER PLUMMER

A Legend

Or

Trick Star

5 Proven Facts about Him you May not Know

....Anderson Gibson....

Table of Contents

Quick Facts

Birthday: December 13, 1929
Nationality: Canadian
Age: 91 Year Old Males
Sun Sign: Sagittarius
Also Known As: Arthur Christopher Orme Plummer
Born In: Toronto, Ontario
Famous As: Actor
Actors Canadian Men
Height: 5'10" (178 cm), 5'10" Males
Spouse/Ex-: Elaine Taylor (M. 1970), Patricia Lewis (M. 1962 – Div. 1967), Tammy Grimes (M. 1956 – Div. 1960)
Father: John Orme Plummer
Mother: Isabella Mary Abbott
Children: Amanda Plummer
City: Toronto, Canada

More Realities

Christopher Plummer is a Canadian entertainer who gained worldwide acknowledgment following his depiction of Aristocrat von Trapp in the super hit melodic film 'The Sound of Music'.

Broadly viewed as one of the best Canadian entertainers, Plummer procured a standing for rejuvenating a few authentic characters on celluloid, including creators Leo Tolstoy and Rudyard Kipling.

He began his vocation on Broadway and worked in a few musicals. Other than his groundbreaking screen presence, it was Plummer's profound and resonant baritone that encouraged him to sack widely praised and grant-winning jobs. He is much of the time related with presumed theater creations, including The Regal Shakespeare Organization and Public Theater.

In the later phase of his vocation, Plummer discovered more accomplishment as his movies became standard hits and gotten rave audits.

With a celebrated lifetime traversing more than fifty years, Plummer has won various honors, including an Oscar, a few Tony grants, and a BAFTA grant. He was additionally respected as the

Buddy of the Request for Canada and later drafted into Canada's Stroll of

Youth and Early Life

Christopher Plummer was brought into the world on December 13, 1929, to Isabella Mary and John Orme Plummer in Toronto, Ontario.

His mom was identified with the Canadian head administrator Sir John Abbott. He grew up with the Abbotts as his folks separated from when he was youthful.

Plummer wished to turn into a piano player and began examining it officially; In any case, he before long found the universe of theater and chose to dive into acting. He went to the Secondary School of Montreal and later McGill College, where he devoted an opportunity to acting.

His initial motivations included Laurence Olivier's 'Henry V'. He later tried the job of Mr. Darcy in his school creation of 'Pride and Bias'.

A neighborhood theater pundit, Herbert Whittaker, observed him and cast him in his creation of 'La Machine Infernale', in 1946.

Vocation

Christopher Plummer's proper presentation on the stage happened in 1953 when he was projected in 'The Starcross Story' at Broadway; in any case, the show didn't perform excessively well. His next exhibition in 'Home is the Legend' was more fruitful and extended to 30 exhibitions.

He made his television debut with the arrangement 'Othello' in 1953 and showed up in a few television arrangements, including 'Studio One', The Alcoa Hour', 'Kraft TV Theater', and 'Meeting with Experience'.

He's featured in the play 'The Dull is Adequately light' alongside Katherine Cornell and Tyrone Force. This show was an extensive achievement and ran from February to April in 1955. They would likewise go on a visit.

In 1955, he featured in the Broadway show, 'Evening of the Auk', inverse Julie Harris and the play, 'J.B.', by Elia Kazan. He procured his first Tony selection for his job in 'J.B.'.

In 1956, he appeared at the Stratford Shakespeare Celebration as Henry in 'Henry V'. The following year, he assumed the fundamental part in 'Hamlet' and a supporting job in 'Twelfth Evening'.

His relationship with the Stratford Shakespeare Celebration proceeded for a long time and he found in 'The Colder time of year's Story', 'A pointless furor about a pointless subject', and 'Romeo and Juliet'.

He made his film debut in 1958 with the film Sidney Lumet's 'Stage Struck'. He next acted in 'Wind Across the Everglades'. His next film appearance was in Anthony Mann's 'The Fall of the Roman Realm'.

He showed up close by Julie Harris in 'Little Moon of Alban', a live television dramatization in 1958. Following the accomplishment of this, he featured in as numerous as 100 television jobs including 'The Moneychangers', 'American Misfortune', 'Our Dads', and 'The Red and the Dark'. He likewise portrayed the energized arrangement 'Madeline'.

Towards the finish of the 1950s, Plummer bit by bit vanished from Broadway shows. He moved to London in the 1960s looking for more work. He was subsequently found in 'The Resistible Ascent of Arturo Ui' and 'The Illustrious Chase of the Sun'.

His relationship with the Illustrious Shakespeare Organization began in 1961 with his part as Benedick in 'A fundamentally nonsensical uproar'. He later played the lead part in 'Richard III' and Lord Henry II in 'Becket'.

His most mainstream job till day is in the Oscar-winning, the record-breaking film 'The Sound of Music' (1965). He played Skipper von Trapp inverse, Julie Andrews. In spite of the overall acknowledgment, Plummer later expressed that he wasn't slanted to assume the part and despised the film.

During the 1960s, he featured in a few different movies including 'Inside Daisy Clover' (1965), 'The evening of the Officers' (1967), The High Magistrate (1968), and 'The Regal Chase of the Sun (1969).

From 1971 to 1972, he was related with Public Venue in London and acted in a few plays. Some of them incorporate Laurence Olivier's 'Amphitryon 38', Jonathan Mill operator's 'Danton's Passing', and 'The Guidelines of the Game'.

He was next found in the melodic 'Cyrano' as the lead character in 1973; His exhibition got him a Tony Grant for Best Entertainer and a Show Work area grant for his remarkable presentation. He likewise played the nominal character in Neil Simon's transformation of Chekov's accounts 'The Acceptable Specialist'.

During the 1980s, his Broadway appearances incorporate 'Othello' and 'Macbeth'. Afterward, he was found in 'A dead zone' and 'Barrymore'.

His part as Mike Wallace the writer in the biographic film 'The Insider' (1999) was exceptionally valued and he got a few honors for this job.

All through the 1990s and 2000s, he was seen in different motion pictures including the hits 'Star Trip VI: The Unfamiliar Nation' (1991), Syriana (2005), and 'Should Cherish Canines (2005).

He denoted his re-visitation of the Stratford Celebration in 2002 with 'Lord Lear', a fruitful creation that was subsequently organized at Lincoln Center in New York.

In 2008, he played Julius Caesar in 'Caesar and Cleopatra' coordinated by Des McAnuff. The play was communicated later in films across Canada. His part in 'The Whirlwind' in 2010 saw a comparative achievement.

In 2012, he showed up in the exclusive show 'A Word or Two' which was a personal excursion where he chronicled his advantage in writing. A spin-off of this 'An Expression of Two Once more' was introduced at the Ahmanson Theater in 2014.

In 2017, he featured in Ridley Scott's 'All the Cash On the

planet', a job initially shot with Kevin Spacey. Plummer's job procured him a Brilliant Globe, Foundation Grant, and BAFTA selections.

Aside from a productive profession as an entertainer, Plummer has effectively worked behind the stage also. He has composed for stage and TV, masterminded music, and performed them too. He stays a functioning piece of the business today.

Significant Works

Plummer's most outstanding job was in the film

'The Sound of Music' (1965).

He would assume the part of Chief von Trapp, while his co-star Julie Andrews played Maria von Trapp.

The film proceeded to break a few records in the cinematic world and has continually been referred to as a foundation in Hollywood film.

Individual Life and Inheritance

Christopher Plummer was hitched to Tammy Grimes, an entertainer, from 1956 to 1960. They had a little girl named Amanda.

He was hitched to Patricia Lewis, a columnist, from 1962 to 1967.

He is right now wedded to Elaine Taylor, an entertainer, since 1970, and a few lives in Weston, Connecticut.

He stays perhaps the most regarded entertainers in Canada. Out of appreciation for his accomplishments, he got the

Canadian Screen Grant for
Lifetime Accomplishment in 2016.

Awards

Institute Awards(Oscars)
2012   Best Execution by an Entertainer in Supporting Role Beginners (2010)

Brilliant Globe Grants
2012   Best Execution by an Entertainer in a Supporting Part in Movement Picture   Beginners (2010)

Early evening Emmy Grants
1994   Outstanding Voice-Over Performance   Madeline (1989)

1994   Outstanding Voice-Over Performance   The New Undertakings of Madeline (1995)

1977   Outstanding Lead
Entertainer in a Restricted Series
Arthur Hailey's the
Moneychangers (1976)

BAFTA Grants
2012   Best Supporting Actor
     Beginners (2010)

Note...............................